The Poetry of Emma
Volume 1

Emma Lazarus was born on July 22nd, 1849, in New York City, the fourth of seven children of Moses Lazarus and Esther Nathan, Sephardic Jews whose families, originally from Portugal, had settled in New York during the colonial period.

From an early age, she studied American and British literature, as well as the German, French, and Italian languages. Her early writings attracted the attention of Ralph Waldo Emerson.

Emma grew to become not only an important poet but also edited many collections of German poems, including Johann Wolfgang von Goethe and Heinrich Heine, some of which we include in these volumes.

Among her other writings are a novel and two plays in five acts, 'The Spagnoletto', a tragic verse drama and 'The Dance to Death', a dramatization of a German short story about the burning of Jews in Nordhausen during the Black Death.

Her interest in her Jewish ancestry grew markedly after reading George Eliot's 'Daniel Deronda', together with the alarming reports of the Russian pogroms following the assassination of Tsar Alexander II in 1881. As a result of this appalling anti-Semitic violence, thousands of destitute Ashkenazi Jews left Russia for New York, leading Lazarus to write articles on the subject as well as the book 'Songs of a Semite' (1882).

She began to help on a more practical level by helping to establish the Hebrew Technical Institute in New York, to provide support, resources and vocational training to help destitute Jewish immigrants become self-supporting.

Emma's best known work is "The New Colossus", a sonnet written in 1883; its lines appear on a bronze plaque in the pedestal of the Statue of Liberty placed there in 1903. It was written for and donated to an auction, conducted by the "Art Loan Fund Exhibition in Aid of the Bartholdi Pedestal Fund for the Statue of Liberty" to raise funds to build the pedestal.

In the latter part of her second trip to Europe (1885 to 1887), she fell seriously ill, it is thought with Hodgkin's lymphoma, and returned to New York City. Emma Lazarus died two months later on November 19, 1887. She is buried in Beth-Olom Cemetery in Brooklyn.

She was an important forerunner of the Zionist movement and argued for the creation of a Jewish homeland thirteen years before Theodor Herzl began to use the term Zionism.

Emma was honored by the Office of the Manhattan Borough President in March 2008 and her home on West 10th Street is included in a map of Women's Rights Historic Sites.

Index Of Poems
The New Colossus
Success
The Supreme Sacrifice
1492

Age And Death
Dreams
Marriage Bells
Fog
Assurance
Destiny
Life and Art
Long Island Sound
City Visions
Influence
Sympathy
Chopin
Florence Nightingale
In the Jewish Synagogue at Newport
In Memoriam—Rev. J. J. Lyons
The Cranes of Ibicus
A June Night
Symphonic Studies (After Schumann)
Critic and Poet: an Epilogue
Venus of the Louvre
The New Ezekiel
The Taming of the Falcon
The Crowing of the Red Cock
Lohengrin: Proem
Exultation
Sonnet
From One Augur to Another
Marjorie's Wooing
Morning
Matins
Song From Heine
Magnetism
The Elixir
St Michael's Chapel
The World's Justice
August Moon
The South
To R.W.E.
Gifts
Epochs
Mater Amabilis
The Birth Of Man
Bar Kochba
The Choice
The Choice
The Valley Of Baca
Links
Youth And Death
Spring Longing
Spring Star
Song

Sunrise
Fra Pedro
Don Rafael
To Carmen Sylva
The Banner Of The Jew
Sic Semper Liberatoribus!

The New Colossus

Not like the brazen giant of Greek fame,
With conquering limbs astride from land to land;
Here at our sea-washed, sunset gates shall stand
A mighty woman with a torch, whose flame
Is the imprisoned lightning, and her name
Mother of Exiles. From her beacon-hand
Glows world-wide welcome; her mild eyes command
The air-bridged harbor that twin cities frame.
"Keep, ancient lands, your storied pomp!" cries she
With silent lips. "Give me your tired, your poor,
Your huddled masses yearning to breathe free,
The wretched refuse of your teeming shore.
Send these, the homeless, tempest-tost to me,
I lift my lamp beside the golden door!"

Success

Oft have I brooded on defeat and pain,
The pathos of the stupid, stumbling throng.
These I ignore to-day and only long
To pour my soul forth in one trumpet strain,
One clear, grief-shattering, triumphant song,
For all the victories of man's high endeavor,
Palm-bearing, laurel deeds that live forever,
The splendor clothing him whose will is strong.
Hast thou beheld the deep, glad eyes of one
Who has persisted and achieved? Rejoice!
On naught diviner shines the all-seeing sun.
Salute him with free heart and choral voice,
'Midst flippant, feeble crowds of spectres wan,
The bold, significant, successful man.

The Supreme Sacrifice

Well-nigh two thousand years hath Israel
Suffered the scorn of man for love of God;
Endured the outlaw's ban, the yoke, the rod,
With perfect patience. Empires rose and fell,
Around him Nebo was adored and Bel;
Edom was drunk with victory, and trod
On his high places, while the sacred sod
Was desecrated by the infidel.
His faith proved steadfast, without breach or flaw,
But now the last renouncement is required.
His truth prevails, his God is God, his Law
Is found the wisdom most to be desired.
Not his the glory! He, maligned, misknown,
Bows his meek head, and says, "Thy will be done!"

1492

Thou two-faced year, Mother of Change and Fate,
Didst weep when Spain cast forth with flaming sword,
The children of the prophets of the Lord,
Prince, priest, and people, spurned by zealot hate.
Hounded from sea to sea, from state to state,
The West refused them, and the East abhorred.
No anchorage the known world could afford,
Close-locked was every port, barred every gate.
Then smiling, thou unveil'dst, O two-faced year,
A virgin world where doors of sunset part,
Saying, "Ho, all who weary, enter here!
There falls each ancient barrier that the art
Of race or creed or rank devised, to rear
Grim bulwarked hatred between heart and heart!"

Age And Death

Come closer, kind, white, long-familiar friend,
Embrace me, fold me to thy broad, soft breast.
Life has grown strange and cold, but thou dost bend
Mild eyes of blessing wooing to my rest.
So often hast thou come, and from my side
So many hast thou lured, I only bide
Thy beck, to follow glad thy steps divine.
Thy world is peopled for me; this world's bare.
Through all these years my couch thou didst prepare.
Thou art supreme Love-kiss me-I am thine!

Dreams

A dream of lilies: all the blooming earth,
A garden full of fairies and of flowers;
Its only music the glad cry of mirth,
While the warm sun weaves golden-tissued hours;
Hope a bright angel, beautiful and true
As Truth herself, and life a lovely toy,
Which ne'er will weary us, ne'er break, a new
Eternal source of pleasure and of joy.

A dream of roses: vision of Loves tree,
Of beauty and of madness, and as bright
As naught on earth save only dreams can be,
Made fair and odorous with flower and light;
A dream that Love is strong to outlast Time,
That hearts are stronger than forgetfulness,
The slippery sand than changeful waves that climb,
The wind-blown foam than mighty waters' stress.

A dream of laurels: after much is gone,
Much buried, much lamented, much forgot,
With what remains to do and what is done,
With what yet is, and what, alas! is not,
Man dreams a dream of laurel and of bays,
A dream of crowns and guerdons and rewards,
Wherein sounds sweet the hollow voice of praise,
And bright appears the wreath that it awards.

A dream of poppies, sad and true as Truth,
That all these dreams were dreams of vanity;
And full of bitter penitence and ruth,
In his last dream, man deems 'twere good to die;
And weeping o'er the visions vain of yore,
In the sad vigils he doth nightly keep,
He dreams it may be good to dream no more,
And life has nothing like Death's dreamless sleep.

Marriage Bells

Music and silver chimes and sunlit air,
Freighted with the scent of honeyed orange-flower;
Glad, friendly festal faces everywhere.
She, rapt from all in this unearthly hour,
With cloudlike, cast-back veil and faint-flushed cheek,
In bridal beauty moves as in a trance
Alone with him, and fears to breathe, to speak,
Lest the rare, subtle spell dissolve perchance.
But he upon that floral head looks down,

Noting the misty eyes, the grave sweet brow--
Doubts if her bliss be perfect as his own,
And dedicates anew with inward vow
His soul unto her service, to repay
Richly the sacrifice she yields this day.

Fog

Light silken curtain, colorless and soft,
Dreamlike before me floating! what abides
Behind thy pearly veil's
Opaque, mysterious woof?

Where sleek red kine, and dappled, crunch day-long
Thick, luscious blades and purple clover-heads,
Nigh me I still can mark
Cool fields of beaded grass.

No more; for on the rim of the globed world
I seem to stand and stare at nothingness.
But songs of unseen birds
And tranquil roll of waves

Bring sweet assurance of continuous life
Beyond this silvery cloud. Fantastic dreams,
Of tissue subtler still
Than the wreathed fog, arise,

And cheat my brain with airy vanishings
And mystic glories of the world beyond.
A whole enchanted town
Thy baffling folds conceal-

An Orient town, with slender-steepled mosques,
Turret from turret springing, dome from dome,
Fretted with burning stones,
And trellised with red gold.

Through spacious streets, where running waters flow,
Sun-screened by fruit-trees and the broad-leaved palm,
Past the gay-decked bazaars,
Walk turbaned, dark-eyed men.

Hark! you can hear the many murmuring tongues,
While loud the merchants vaunt their gorgeous wares.
The sultry air is spiced
With fragrance of rich gums,

And through the lattice high in yon dead wall,

See where, unveiled, an arch, young, dimpled face,
Flushed like a musky peach,
Peers down upon the mart!

From her dark, ringleted and bird-poised head
She hath cast back the milk-white silken veil:
'Midst the blank blackness there
She blossoms like a rose.

Beckons she not with those bright, full-orbed eyes,
And open arms that like twin moonbeams gleam?
Behold her smile on me
With honeyed, scarlet lips!

Divine Scheherazade! I am thine.
I come! I come!-Hark! from some far-off mosque
The shrill muezzin calls
The hour of silent prayer,

And from the lattice he hath scared my love.
The lattice vanisheth itself-the street,
The mart, the Orient town;
Only through still, soft air

That cry is yet prolonged. I wake to hear
The distant fog-horn peal: before mine eyes
Stands the white wall of mist,
Blending with vaporous skies.

Elusive gossamer, impervious
Even to the mighty sun-god's keen red shafts!
With what a jealous art
Thy secret thou dost guard!

Well do I know deep in thine inmost folds,
Within an opal hollow, there abides
The lady of the mist,
The Undine of the air

A slender, winged, ethereal, lily form,
Dove-eyed, with fair, free-floating, pearl-wreathed hair,
In waving raiment swathed
Of changing, irised hues.

Where her feet, rosy as a shell, have grazed
The freshened grass, a richer emerald glows:
Into each flower-cup
Her cool dews she distills.

She knows the tops of jagged mountain-peaks,
She knows the green soft hollows of their sides,

And unafraid she floats
O'er the vast-circled seas.

She loves to bask within the moon's wan beams,
Lying, night-long upon the moist, dark earth,
And leave her seeded pearls
With morning on the grass.

Ah! that athwart these dim, gray outer courts
Of her fantastic palace I might pass,
And reach the inmost shrine
Of her chaste solitude,

And feel her cool and dewy fingers press
My mortal-fevered brow, while in my heart
She poured with tender love
Her healing Lethe-balm!

See! the close curtain moves, the spell dissolves!
Slowly it lifts: the dazzling sunshine streams
Upon a newborn world
And laughing summer seas.

Swift, snowy-breasted sandbirds twittering glance
Through crystal air. On the horizon's marge,
Like a huge purple wraith,
The dusky fog retreats.

Assurance

Last night I slept, and when I woke her kiss
Still floated on my lips. For we had strayed
Together in my dream, through some dim glade,
Where the shy moonbeams scarce dared light our bliss.
The air was dank with dew, between the trees,
The hidden glow-worms kindled and were spent.
Cheek pressed to cheek, the cool, the hot night-breeze
Mingled ouir hair, our breath, and came and went,
As sporting with our passion. Low and deep
Spake in mine ear her voice: "And didst thou dream,
This could be buried? This could be sleep?
And love be thrall to death! Nay, whatso seem,
Have faith, dear heart; this is the thing that is!"
Thereon I woke, and on my lips her kiss.

Destiny

1856

Paris, from throats of iron, silver, brass,
Joy-thundering cannon, blent with chiming bells,
And martial strains, the full-voiced pæan swells.
The air is starred with flags, the chanted mass
Throngs all the churches, yet the broad streets swarm
With glad-eyed groups who chatter, laugh, and pass,
In holiday confusion, class with class.
And over all the spring, the sun-floods warm!
In the Imperial palace that March morn,
The beautiful young mother lay and smiled;
For by her side just breathed the Prince, her child,
Heir to an empire, to the purple born,
Crowned with the Titan's name that stirs the heart
Like a blown clarion--one more Bonaparte.

1879

Born to the purple, lying stark and dead,
Transfixed with poisoned spears, beneath the sun
Of brazen Africa! Thy grave is one,
Fore-fated youth (on whom were visited
Follies and sins not thine), whereat the world,
Heartless howe'er it be, will pause to sing
A dirge, to breathe a sigh, a wreath to fling
Of rosemary and rue with bay-leaves curled.
Enmeshed in toils ambitious, not thine own,
Immortal, loved boy-Prince, thou tak'st thy stand
With early doomed Don Carlos, hand in hand
With mild-browed Arthur, Geoffrey's murdered son.
Louis the Dauphin lifts his thorn-ringed head,
And welcomes thee, his brother, 'mongst the dead.

Life and Art

Not while the fever of the blood is strong,
The heart throbs loud, the eyes are veiled, no less
With passion than with tears, the Muse shall bless
The poet-sould to help and soothe with song.
Not then she bids his trembling lips express
The aching gladness, the voluptuous pain.
Life is his poem then; flesh, sense, and brain
One full-stringed lyre attuned to happiness.
But when the dream is done, the pulses fail,
The day's illusion, with the day's sun set,
He, lonely in the twilight, sees the pale
Divine Consoler, featured like Regret,

Enter and clasp his hand and kiss his brow.
Then his lips ope to sing--as mine do now.

Long Island Sound

I see it as it looked one afternoon
In August,-by a fresh soft breeze o'erblown.
The swiftness of the tide, the light thereon,
A far-off sail, white as a crescent moon.
The shining waters with pale currents strewn,
The quiet fishing-smacks, the Eastern cove,
The semi-circle of its dark, green grove.
The luminous grasses, and the merry sun
In the grave sky; the sparkle far and wide,
Laughter of unseen children, cheerful chirp
Of crickets, and low lisp of rippling tide,
Light summer clouds fantastical as sleep
Changing unnoted while I gazed thereon.
All these fair sounds and sights I made my own.

City Visions

I

As the blind Milton's memory of light,
The deaf Beethoven's phantasy of tone,
Wroght joys for them surpassing all things known
In our restricted sphere of sound and sight,--
So while the glaring streets of brick and stone
Vix with heat, noise, and dust from morn till night,
I will give rein to Fancy, taking flight
From dismal now and here, and dwell alone
With new-enfranchised senses. All day long,
Think ye 't is I, who sit 'twixt darkened walls,
While ye chase beauty over land and sea?
Uplift on wings of some rare poet's song
Where the wide billow laughs and leaps and falls,
I soar cloud-high, free as the winds are free.

II

Who grasps the substance? who 'mid shadows strays?
He who within some dark-bright wood reclines,
'Twixt sleep and waking, where the needled pines
Have cushioned al his couch with soft brown sprays?
He notes not how the living water shines,
Trembling along the cliff, a flickering haze,
Brimming a wine-bright pool, nor lifts his gaze

To read the ancient wonders and the signs.
Does he possess the actual, or do I,
Who paint on air more than his sense receives,
The glittering pine-tufts with closed eyes behold,
Breathe the strong resinous perfume, see the sky
Quiver like azure flame between the leaves,
And open unseen gates with key of gold?

Influence

The fervent, pale-faced Mother ere she sleep,
Looks out upon the zigzag-lighted square,
The beautiful bare trees, the blue night-air,
The revelation of the star-strewn deep,
World above world, and heaven over heaven.
Between the tree-tops and the skies, her sight
Rests on a steadfast, ruddy-shining light,
High in the tower, an earthly star of even.
Hers is the faith in saints' and angels' power,
And mediating love--she breathes a prayer
For yon tired watcher in the gray old tower.
He the shrewd, skeptic poet unaware
Feels comforted and stilled, and knows not whence
Falls this unwonted peace on heart and sense.

Sympathy

Therefore I dare reveal my private woe,
The secret blots of my imperfect heart,
Nor strive to shrink or swell mine own desert,
Nor beautify nor hide. For this I know,
That even as I am, thou also art.
Thou past heroic forms unmoved shalt go,
To pause and bide with me, to whisper low:
"Not I alone am weak, not I apart
Must suffer, struggle, conquer day by day.
Here is my very cross by strangers borne,
Here is my bosom-sin wherefrom I pray
Hourly deliverance--this my rose, my thorn.
This woman my soul's need can understand,
Stretching o'er silent gulfs her sister hand."

Chopin

I

A dream of interlinking hands, of feet
Tireless to spin the unseen, fairy woof
Of the entangling waltz. Bright eyebeams meet,
Gay laughter echoes from the vaulted roof.
Warm perfumes rise; the soft unflickering glow
Of branching lights sets off the changeful charms
Of glancing gems, rich stuffs, the dazzling snow
Of necks unkerchieft, and bare, clinging arms.
Hark to the music! How beneath the strain
Of reckless revelry, vibrates and sobs
One fundamental chord of constant pain,
The pulse-beat of the poet's heart that throbs.
So yearns, though all the dancing waves rejoice,
The troubled sea's disconsolate, deep voice.

II

Who shall proclaim the golden fable false
Of Orpheus' miracles? This subtle strain
Above our prose-world's sordid loss and gain
Lightly uplifts us. With the rhythmic waltz,
The lyric prelude, the nocturnal song
Of love and languor, varied visions rise,
That melt and blend to our enchanted eyes.
The Polish poet who sleeps silenced long,
The seraph-souled musician, breathes again
Eternal eloquence, immortal pain.
Revived the exalted face we know so well,
The illuminated eyes, the fragile frame,
Slowly consuming with its inward flame,
We stir not, speak not, lest we break the spell.

III

A voice was needed, sweet and true and fine
As the sad spirit of the evening breeze,
Throbbing with human passion, yet devine
As the wild bird's untutored melodies.
A voice for him 'neath twilight heavens dim,
Who mourneth for his dead, while round him fall
The wan and noiseless leaves. A voice for him
Who sees the first green sprout, who hears the call
Of the first robin on the first spring day.
A voice for all whom Fate hath set apart,
Who, still misprized, must perish by the way,
Longing with love, for that they lack the art
Of their own soul's expression. For all these
Sing the unspoken hope, the vague, sad reveries.

IV

Then Nature shaped a poet's heart--a lyre
From out whose chords the lightest breeze that blows
Drew trembling music, wakening sweet desire.
How shall she cherish him? Behold! she throws
This precious, fragile treasure in the whirl
Of seething passions; he is scourged and stung,
Must dive in storm-vext seas, if but one pearl
Of art or beauty therefrom may be wrung.
No pure-browed pensive nymph his Muse shall be,
An amazon of thought with sovereign eyes,
Whose kiss was poison, man-brained, worldy-wise,
Inspired that elfin, delicate harmony.
Rich gain for us! But with him is it well?
The poet who must sound earth, heaven, and hell!

Florence Nightingale

Upon the whitewashed walls
A woman's shadow falls,
A woman walketh o'er the darksome floors.
A soft, angelic smile
Lighteth her face the while,
In passing through the dismal corridors.

And now and then there slips
A word from out her lips,
More sweet and grateful to those listening ears
Than the most plaintive tale
Of the sad nightingale,
Whose name and tenderness this woman bears.

Her presence in the room
Of agony and gloom,
No fretful murmurs, no coarse words profane;
For while she standeth there,
All words are hushed save prayer;
She seems God's angel weeping o'er man's pain.

And some of them arise,
With eager, tearful eyes,
From off their couch to see her passing by.
Some, e'en too weak for this,
Can only stoop and kiss
Her shadow, and fall back content to die.

No monument of stone
Needs this heroic one,
Her name is graven on each noble heart;
And in all after years

Her praise will be the tears
Which at that name from quivering lids will start.

And those who live not now,
To see the sainted brow,
And the angelic smile before it flits for aye,
They in the future age
Will kiss the storied page
Whereon the shadow of her life will lie.

In the Jewish Synagogue at Newport

Here, where the noises of the busy town,
The ocean's plunge and roar can enter not,
We stand and gaze around with tearful awe,
And muse upon the consecrated spot.

No signs of life are here: the very prayers
Inscribed around are in a language dead;
The light of the "perpetual lamp" is spent
That an undying radiance was to shed.

What prayers were in this temple offered up,
Wrung from sad hearts that knew no joy on earth,
By these lone exiles of a thousand years,
From the fair sunrise land that gave them birth!

How as we gaze, in this new world of light,
Upon this relic of the days of old,
The present vanishes, and tropic bloom
And Eastern towns and temples we behold.

Again we see the patriarch with his flocks,
The purple seas, the hot blue sky o'erhead,
The slaves of Egypt, omens, mysteries,
Dark fleeing hosts by flaming angels led.

A wondrous light upon a sky-kissed mount,
A man who reads Jehovah's written law,
'Midst blinding glory and effulgence rare,
Unto a people prone with reverent awe.

The pride of luxury's barbaric pomp,
In the rich court of royal Solomon
Alas! we wake: one scene alone remains,
The exiles by the streams of Babylon.

Our softened voices send us back again
But mournful echoes through the empty hall:

Our footsteps have a strange unnatural sound,
And with unwonted gentleness they fall.

The weary ones, the sad, the suffering,
All found their comfort in the holy place,
And children's gladness and men's gratitude
'Took voice and mingled in the chant of praise.

The funeral and the marriage, now, alas!
We know not which is sadder to recall;
For youth and happiness have followed age,
And green grass lieth gently over all.

Nathless the sacred shrine is holy yet,
With its lone floors where reverent feet once trod.
Take off your shoes as by the burning bush,
Before the mystery of death and God.

In Memoriam—Rev. J. J. Lyons

ROSH-HASHANAH, 5638.

The golden harvest-tide is here, the corn
Bows its proud tops beneath the reaper's hand.
Ripe orchards' plenteous yields enrich the land;
Bring the first fruits and offer them this morn,
With the stored sweetness of all summer hours,
The amber honey sucked from myriad flowers,
And sacrifice your best first fruits to-day,
With fainting hearts and hands forespent with toil,
Offer the mellow harvest's splendid spoil,
To Him who gives and Him who takes away.

Bring timbrels, bring the harp of sweet accord,
And in a pleasant psalm your voice attune,
And blow the cornet greeting the new moon.
Sing, holy, holy, holy, is the Lord,
Who killeth and who quickeneth again,
Who woundeth and who healeth mortal pain,
Whose hand afflicts us, and who sends us peace.
Hail thou slim arc of promise in the West,
Thou pledge of certain plenty, peace, and rest.
With the spent year, may the year's sorrows cease.

For there is mourning now in Israel,
The crown, the garland of the branching tree
Is plucked and withered. Ripe of years was he.
The priest, the good old man who wrought so well
Upon his chosen globe. For he was one

Who at his seed-plot toiled through rain and sun.
Morn found him not as one who slumbereth,
Noon saw him faithful, and the restful night
Stole o'er him at his labors to requite
The just man's service with the just man's death.

What shall be said when such as he do pass?
Go to the hill-side, neath the cypress trees,
Fall midst that peopled silence on your knees,
And weep that man must wither as the grass.
But mourn him not, whose blameless life complete
Rounded its perfect orb, whose sleep is sweet,
Whom we must follow, but may not recall.
Salute with solemn trumpets the New Year,
And offer honeyed fruits as were he here,
Though ye be sick with wormwood and with gall.

The Cranes of Ibicus

Here was a man who watched the river flow
Past the huge town, one gray November day.
Round him in narrow high-piled streets at play
The boys made merry as they saw him go,
Murmuring half-loud, with eyes upon the stream,
The immortal screed he held within his hand.
For he was walking in an April land
With Faust and Helen. Shadowy as a dream
Was the prose-world, the river and the town.
Wild joy possessed him; through enchanted skies
He saw the cranes of Ibycus swoop down.
He closed the page, he lifted up his eyes,
Lo - a black line of birds in wavering thread
Bore him the greetings of the deathless dead!

A June Night

Ten o'clock: the broken moon
Hangs not yet a half hour high,
Yellow as a shield of brass,
In the dewy air of June,
Poised between the vaulted sky
And the ocean's liquid glass.

Earth lies in the shadow still;
Low black bushes, trees, and lawn
Night's ambrosial dews absorb;
Through the foliage creeps a thrill,

Whispering of yon spectral dawn
And the hidden climbing orb.

Higher, higher, gathering light,
Veiling with a golden gauze
All the trembling atmosphere,
See, the rayless disk grows white!
Hark, the glittering billows pause!

Faint, far sounds possess the ear.
Elves on such a night as this
Spin their rings upon the grass;
On the beach the water-fay
Greets her lover with a kiss;
Through the air swift spirits pass,
Laugh, caress, and float away.

Shut thy lids and thou shalt see
Angel faces wreathed with light,
Mystic forms long vanished hence.
Ah, too fine, too rare, they be
For the grosser mortal sight,
And they foil our waking sense.

Yet we feel them floating near,
Know that we are not alone,
Though our open eyes behold
Nothing save the moon's bright sphere,
In the vacant heavens shown,
And the ocean's path of gold.

Symphonic Studies (After Schumann)

Prelude
Blue storm-clouds in hot heavens of mid-July
Hung heavy, brooding over land and sea:
Our hearts, a-tremble, throbbed in harmony
With the wild, restless tone of air and sky.
Shall we not call im Prospero who held
In his enchanted hands the fateful key
Of that tempestuous hour's mystery,
And with controlling wand our spirits spelled,
With him to wander by a sun-bright shore,
To hear fine, fairy voices, and to fly
With disembodied Ariel once more
Above earth's wrack and ruin? Far and nigh
The laughter of the thunder echoed loud,
And harmless lightnings leapt from cloud to cloud.

I

Floating upon a swelling wave of sound,
We seemed to overlook an endless sea:
Poised 'twixt clear heavens and glittering surf were we.
We drank the air in flight: we knew no bound
To the audacious ventures of desire.
Nigh us the sun was dropping, drowned in gold;
Deep, deep below the burning billows rolled;
And all the sea sang like a smitten lyre.
Oh, the wild voices of those chanting waves!
The human faces glimpsed beneath the tide!
Familiar eyes gazed from profound sea-caves,
And we, exalted, were as we had died.
We knew the sea was Life, the harmonious cry
The blended discords of humanity.

II

Look deeper yet: mark 'midst the wave-blurred mass,
In lines distinct, in colors clear defined,
The typic groups and figures of mankind.
Behold within the cool and liquid glass
Bright child-folk sporting with smooth yellow shells,
Astride of dolphins, leaping up to kiss
Fair mother-faces. From the vast abyss
How joyously their thought-free laughter wells!
Some slumber in grim caverns unafraid,
Lulled by the overwhelming water's sound,
And some make mouths at dragons, undismayed.
Oh dauntless innocence! The gulfs profound
Reëcho strangely with their ringing glee,
And with wise mermaids' plaintive melody.

III

What do the sea-nymphs in that coral cave?
With wondering eyes their supple forms they bend
O'er something rarely beautiful. They lend
Their lithe white arms, and through the golden wave
They lift it tenderly. Oh blinding sight!
A naked, radiant goddess, tranced in sleep,
Full-limbed, voluptuous, 'neath the mantling sweep
Of auburn locks that kiss her ankles white!
Upward they bear her, chanting low and sweet:
The clinging waters part before their way,
Jewels of flame are dancing 'neath their feet.
Up in the sunshine, on soft foam, they lay
Their precious burden, and return forlorn.
Oh, bliss! oh, anguish! Mortals, Love is born!

IV

Hark! from unfathomable deeps a dirge
Swells sobbing through the melancholy air:

Where love has entered, Death is also there.
The wail outrings the chafed, tumultuous surge;
Ocean and earth, the illimitable skies,
Prolong one note, a mourning for the dead,
The cry of souls not to be comforted.
What piercing music! Funeral visions rise,
And send the hot tears raining down our cheek.
We see the silent grave upon the hill
With its lone lilac-bush. O heart, be still!
She will not rise, she will not stir nor speak.
Surely, the unreturning dead are blest.
Ring on, sweet dirge, and knell us to our rest!

V
Upon the silver beach the undines dance
With interlinking arms and flying hair;
Like polished marble gleam their limbs left bare;
Upon their virgin rites pale moonbeams glance.
Softer the music! for their foam-bright feet
Print not the moist floor where they trip their round:
Affrighted they will scatter at a sound,
Leap in their cool sea-chambers, nibly fleet,
And we shall doubt that we have ever seen,
While our sane eyes behold stray wreaths of mist,
Shot with faint colors by the moon-rays kissed,
Floating snow-soft, snow-white, where these had been.
Already, look! the wave-washed sands are bare,
And mocking laughter ripples through the air.

VI
Divided 'twixt the dream-world and the real,
We heard the waxing passion of the song
Soar as to scale the heavens on pinions strong.
Amidst the long-reverberant thunder-peal,
Against the rain-blurred square of light, the head
Of the pale poet at the lyric keys
Stood boldly cut, absorbed in reveries,
While over it keen-bladed lightnings played.
"Rage on, wild storm!" the music seemed to sing:
"Not all the thunders of thy wrath can move
The soul that's dedicate to worshipping
Eternal Beauty, everlasting Love."
No more! the song was ended, and behold,
A rainbow trembling on a sky of gold!

Epilogue
Forth in the sunlit, rain-bathed air we stepped,
Sweet with the dripping grass and flowering vine,
And saw through irised clouds the pale sun shine.
Back o'er the hills the rain-mist slowly crept

Like a transparent curtain's silvery sheen;
And fronting us the painted bow was arched,
Whereunder the majestic cloud-shapes marched:
In the wet, yellow light the dazzling green
Of lawn and bush and tree seemed stained with blue.
Our hearts o'erflowed with peace. With smiles we spake
Of partings in the past, of courage new,
Of high achievement, of the dreams that make
A wonder and a glory of our days,
And all life's music but a hymn of praise.

Critic and Poet: an Epilogue

("Poetry must be simple, sensuous, or impassioned; this man is neither simple, sensuous, nor impassioned; therefore he is not a poet")

No man had ever heard a nightingale,
When once a keen-eyed naturalist was stirred
To study and define what is a bird,
To classify by rote and book, nor fail
To mark its structure and to note the scale
Whereon its song might possibly be heard.
Thus far, no farther; so he spake the word.
When of a sudden, hark, the nightingale!

Oh deeper, higher than he could divine
That all-unearthly, untaught strain! He saw
The plain, brown warbler, unabashed. "Not mine"
(He cried) "the error of this fatal flaw.
No bird is this, it soars beyond my line,
Were it a bird, 'twould answer to my law."

Venus of the Louvre

Down the long hall she glistens like a star,
The foam-born mother of Love, transfixed to stone,
Yet none the less immortal, breathing on.
Time's brutal hand hath maimed but could not mar.
When first the enthralled enchantress from afar
Dazzled mine eyes, I saw not her alone,
Serenely poised on her world-worshipped throne,
As when she guided once her dove-drawn car,
But at her feet a pale, death-stricken Jew,
Her life adorer, sobbed farewell to love.
Here Heine wept! Here still he weeps anew,
Nor ever shall his shadow lift or move,
While mourns one ardent heart, one poet-brain,

For vanished Hellas and Hebraic plain.

The New Ezekiel

What, can these dead bones live, whose sap is dried
By twenty scorching centuries of wrong?
Is this the House of Israel, whose pride
Is as a tale that's told, an ancient song?
Are these ignoble relics all that live
Of psalmist, priest, and prophet? Can the breath
Of very heaven bid these bones revive,
Open the graves and clothe the ribs of death?

Yea, Prophesy, the Lord hath said. Again
Say to the wind, Come forth and breathe afresh,
Even that they may live upon these slain,
And bone to bone shall leap, and flesh to flesh.
The Spirit is not dead, proclaim the word,
Where lay dead bones, a host of armed men stand!
I ope your graves, my people, saith the Lord,
And I shall place you living in your land.

The Taming of the Falcon

The bird sits spelled upon the lithe brown wrist
Of yonder turbaned fowler, who had lamed
No feather limb, but the winged spirit tamed
With his compelling eye. He need not trust
The silken coil, not set the thick-limed snare;
He lures the wanderer with his steadfast gaze,
It shrinks, it quails, it trembles yet obeys.
And, lo! he has enslaved the thing of air.
The fixed, insistent human will is lord
Of all the earth; but in the awful sky
Reigns absolute, unreached by deed or word
Above creation; through eternity,
Outshining the sun's shield, the lightening's sword,
The might of Allah's unaverted eye.

The Crowing of the Red Cock

Across the Eastern sky has glowed
The flicker of a blood-red dawn,
Once more the clarion cock has crowed,
Once more the sword of Christ is drawn.

A million burning rooftrees light
The world-wide path of Israel's flight.

Where is the Hebrew's fatherland?
The folk of Christ is sore bestead;
The Son of Man is bruised and banned,
Nor finds whereon to lay his head.
His cup is gall, his meat is tears,
His passion lasts a thousand years.

Each crime that wakes in man the beast,
Is visited upon his kind.
The lust of mobs, the greed of priest,
The tyranny of kings, combined
To root his seed from earth again,
His record is one cry of pain.

When the long roll of Christian guilt
Against his sires and kin is known,
The flood of tears, the life-blood spilt,
The agony of ages shown,
What oceans can the stain remove,
From Christian law and Christian love?

Nay, close the book; not now, not here,
The hideous tale of sin narrate,
Reëchoing in the martyr's ear,
Even he might nurse revengeful hate,
Even he might turn in wrath sublime,
With blood for blood and crime for crime.

Coward? Not he, who faces death,
Who singly against worlds has fought,
For what? A name he may not breathe,
For liberty of prayer and thought.
The angry sword he will not whet,
His nobler task is - to forget.

Lohengrin: Proem

The alert and valiant faith that could respond,
Upon life's threshold, to the highest call,
Unquestioning of what might lie beyond,
Courage afield and courtesy in hall,
And sweet, unbroken patience therewithal,
And simple loyalty, can these things be
The virtues that have died with chivalry?

The lapsing stream that leads to love and fate,

Now mystic-shadowed, and now broad and free,
Reflecting all the gold of heaven's gate;
The snowy bird's symbolic purity,
The toilsome contest and the victory,
The troubled joy of life, and after these,
The crowning guerdon of the perfect peace,

These dreams have filled my dazzled sense and brain,
With images so vivid that at last
I wake to life and find them all again
Repeated in the present as the past,
The hues recolored and the forms recast;
And in familiar eyes I see outshine
The old heroic faith in love divine.

No empty fable of a day long dead,
No baseless vision of some sanguine saint,
No legend, only half rememberéd,
Of prowess obsolete and virtues quaint;
But be this rather a reflection faint
Of that which taught me how the near and real
Surpass in strength and beauty the ideal.

Exultation

Behold, I walked abroad at early morning,
The fields of June were bathed in dew and lustre,
The hills were clad with light as with a garment.

The inexpressible auroral freshness,
The grave, immutable, aerial heavens,
The transient clouds above the quiet landscape,

The heavy odor of the passionate lilacs,
That hedged the road with sober-colored clusters,
All these o'ermastered me with subtle power,

And made my rural walk a royal progress,
Peopled my solitude with airy spirits,
Who hovered over me with joyous singing.

'Behold!' they sang, 'the glory of the morning.
Through every vein does not the summer tingle,
With vague desire and flush of expectation?

'To think how fair is life! set round with grandeur;
The eloquent sea beneath the voiceless heavens,
The shifting shows of every bounteous season;

'Rich skies, fantastic clouds, and herby meadows,
Gray rivers, prairies spread with regal flowers,
Grasses and grains and herds of browsing cattle:

'Great cities filled with breathing men and women,
Of whom the basest have their aspirations,
High impulses of courage or affection.

'And on this brave earth still those finer spirits,
Heroic Valor, admirable Friendship,
And Love itself, a very god among you.

'All these for thee, and thou evoked from nothing,
Born from blank darkness to this blaze of beauty,
Where is thy faith, and where are thy thanksgivings?'

The world is his who can behold it rightly,
Who hears the harmonies of unseen angels
Above the senseless outcry of the hour.

Sonnet

Stil northward is the central mount of Maine,
From whose high crown the rugged forests seem
Like shaven lawns, and lakes with frequent gleam,
'Like broken mirrors,' flash back light again.
Eastward the sea, with its majestic plain,
Endless, of radiant, restless blue, superb
With might and music, whether storms perturb
Its reckless waves, or halcyon winds that reign,
Make it serene as wisdom. Storied Spain
Is the next coast, and yet we may not sigh
For lands beyond the inexorable main;
Our noble scenes have yet no history.
All subtler charms than those that feed the eye,
Our lives must give them; 'tis an aim austere,
But opes new vistas, and a pathway clear.

From One Augur to Another

So, Calchas, on the sacred Palatine,
You thought of Mopsus, and o'er wastes of sea
A flower brought your message. I divine
(Through my deep art) the kindly mockery
That played about your lips and in your eyes,
Plucking the frail leaf, while you dreamed of home.
Thanks for the silent greeting! I shall prize,

Beyond June's rose, the scentless flower of Rome.
All the Campagna spreads before my sight,
The mouldering wall, the Caesars' tombs unwreathed,
Rome and the Tiber, and the yellow light,
Wherein the honey-colored blossom breathed.
But most I thank it - egoists that we be!
For proving then and there you thought of me.

Marjorie's Wooing

The corn was yellow upon the cliffs,
The fluttering grass was green to see,
The waves were blue as the sky above,
And the sun it was shining merrily.

'Marjorie, Marjorie! do you love me,
Faithfully, truly as I love you?'
The little lass reddened, and whitened, and smiled,
And answered him with her clear eyes of blue.

'Marjorie, you are but gentle and young;
I am too old and too rough for you.'
The little lass, trustfully giving her hand,
Answered, 'I love you, faithful and true.'

'Marjorie, Marjorie, when shall we wed?'
'As soon as you will it, to-morrow, to-day.'
'Marjorie, Marjorie, if you knew all,
Would you still say me the words that you say?'

'If I knew all?' said the little lass,
'I know you are Kenneth, the brave and strong;
I know that I love, and that you are good:
I will know it e'er, and have known it long.'

'Marjorie, Marjorie, if I should say
I fled from prison to come to you;
I stabbed a man all for jealous love;
I am not noble, nor good, nor true?'

'Kenneth, your eyes would belie your words,'
Boldly and bravely the lass replied.
'Why should God fill them with love and truth,
And your heart with cruelty, hate, and pride?'

'Marjorie, Marjorie, if I should say
That I loved many ere I loved you?'
'Ere you had seen me,' Marjorie said,
' How could you know I was loving and true?'

'Marjorie, Marjorie, if I should say
That I was outcast on land and on sea?'
'All the more reason,' the little maid said,
' Why you should ever be loved by me.'

'Marjorie, Marjorie, if I should say
That I was noble, and titled, and grand;
Lord of the woods, and the castle, and park,
Lord of the acres of corn o'er the land?'

Dropping a courtesy, the little lass said,
'Still should I love you and ever be true;
But if you found me too lowly and poor,
I should bid farewell and go die for you.'

'Marjorie, darling, I tell you then,
This is the truth, and the land is mine,
And the castle, the park, and the vessel far off,
And whatever is mine, is thine, dear, thine!'

Morning

Gray-vested Dawn, with flameless, tranquil eye,
Cool hands, and dewy lips, is in the sky,
A sober nun, with starry rosary.

With eyes downcast and with uplifted palm,
She seems to whisper now her silent psalm;
Beneath her gaze the sleeping earth is calm.

Her prayer is ended, and she riseth slow,
And o'er the hills she quietly doth go,
Noiseless and gentle as the midnight snow.

Then suddenly the pale-east blushes red,
The flowers to see upraise a sleepy head,
The rosy colors deepen, grow, and spread.

A cool breeze whispers: 'She is coming now!'
And then the radiant colors burn and glow,
The white cast blushes over cheek and brow,

And glorious on the hills the Morning stands,
Her saffron hair back-blown from rosy bands,
And light and joy and fragrance in her hands.

Her foot has touched the hill-tops, and they shine;
She comes, the willow rustles and the pine;

She smiles upon the fields a smile divine,

And all the earth smiles back; from mount to vale,
From oak to shuddering grass, from glen to dale,
Wet fields and flowers and glistening brooks cry 'Hail!'

Matins

Gray earth, gray mist, gray sky:
Through vapors hurrying by,
Larger than wont, on high
Floats the horned, yellow moon.
Chill airs are faintly stirred,
And far away is heard,
Of some fresh-awakened bird,
The querulous, shrill tune.

The dark mist hides the face
Of the dim land: no trace
Of rock or river's place
In the thick air is drawn;
But dripping grass smells sweet,
And rustling branches meet,
And sounding water greet
The slow, sure, sacred dawn.

Past is the long black night,
With its keen lightnings white,
Thunder and floods: new light
The glimmering low east streaks.
The dense clouds part: between
Their jagged rents are seen
Pale reaches blue and green,
As the mirk curtain breaks.

Above the shadowy world,
Still more and more unfurled,
The gathered mists upcurled
Like phantoms melt and pass.
In clear-obscure revealed,
Brown wood, gray stream, dark field:
Fresh, healthy odors yield
Wet furrows, flowers, and grass.

The sudden, splendid gleam
Of one thin, golden beam
Shoots from the feathered rim
Of yon hill crowned with woods.
Down its embowered side,

As living waters slide,
So the great morning tide
Follows in sunny floods.

From bush and hedge and tree
Joy, unrestrained and free,
Breaks forth in melody,
Twitter and chirp and song:
Alive the festal air
With gauze-winged creatures fair,
That flicker everywhere,
Dart, poise, and flash along.

The shining mists are gone,
Slight films of gold swift-blown
Before the strong, bright sun
Or the deep-colored sky:
A world of life and glow
Sparkles and basks below,
Where the soft meads a-row,
Hoary with dew-fall, lie.

Does not the morn break thus,
Swift, bright, victorious,
With new skies cleared for us,
Over the soul storm-tost?
Her night was long and deep,
Strange visions vexed her sleep,
Strange sorrows bade her weep:
Her faith in dawn was lost.

No halt, no rest for her,
The immortal wanderer
From sphere to higher sphere,
Toward the pure source of day.
The new light shames her fears,
Her faithlessness, her tears,
As the new sun appears
To light her godlike way.

Song From Heine

My heart, my heart is heavy,
Though merrily blooms the May;
Out on the ancient bastion,
Under the lindens I stay.
There stands by yon gray old tower,
The sentry-house of the town;
A red clad peasant soldier

Goes pacing up and down.
He toys with his shining musket,
That gleams in the sunset red,
Presenting and shouldering arms now,
I wish he would shoot me dead!

Magnetism

By the impulse of my will,
By the red flame in my blood,
By me nerves' electric thrill,
By the passion of my mood,
My concentrated desire,
My undying, desperate love,
I ignore Fate, I defy her,
Iron-hearted Death I move.
When the town lies numb with sleep,
Here, round-eyed I sit; my breath
Quickly stirred, my flesh a-creep,
And I force the gates of death.
I nor move nor speak-you'd deem
From my quiet face and hands,
I were tranced but in her dream,
SHE responds, she understands.
I have power on what is not,
Or on what has ceased to be,
From that deep, earth-hollowed spot,
I can lift her up to me.
And, or ere I am aware
Through the closed and curtained door,
Comes my lady white and fair,
And embraces me once more.
Though the clay clings to her gown,
Yet all heaven is in her eyes;
Cool, kind fingers press mine eyes,
To my soul her soul replies.
But when breaks the common dawn,
And the city wakes - behold!
My shy phantom is withdrawn,
And I shiver lone and cold.
And I know when she has left,
She is stronger far than I,
And more subtly spun her weft,
Than my human wizardry.
Though I force her to my will,
By the red flame in my blood,
By my nerves' electric thrill,
By the passion of my mood,
Yet all day a ghost am I.

Nerves unstrung, spent will, dull brain.
I achieve, attain, but die,
And she claims me hers again.

The Elixir

'Oh brew me a potion strong and good!
One golden drop in his wine
Shall charm his sense and fire his blood,
And bend his will to mine.'

Poor child of passion! ask of me
Elixir of death or sleep,
Or Lethe's stream; but love is free,
And woman must wait and weep.

St Michael's Chapel

When the vexed hubbub of our world of gain
Roars round about me as I walk the street,
The myriad noise of Traffic, and the beat
Of Toil's incessant hammer, the fierce strain
Of struggle hand to hand and brain to brain,
Ofttimes a sudden dream my sense will cheat,
The gaudy shops, the sky-piled roofs retreat,
And all at once I stand enthralled again
Within a marble minster over-seas.
I watch the solemn gold-stained gloom that creeps
To kiss an alabaster tomb, where sleeps
A lady 'twixt two knights' stone effigies,
And every day in dusky glory steeps
Their sculptured slumber of five centuries.

The World's Justice

If the sudden tidings came
That on some far, foreign coast,
Buried ages long from fame,
Had been found a remnant lost
Of that hoary race who dwelt
By the golden Nile divine,
Spake the Pharaoh's tongue and knelt
At the moon-crowned Isis' shrine
How at reverend Egypt's feet,
Pilgrims from all lands would meet!

If the sudden news were known,
That anigh the desert-place
Where once blossomed Babylon,
Scions of a mighty race
Still survived, of giant build,
Huntsmen, warriors, priest and sage,
Whose ancestral fame had filled,
Trumpet-tongued, the earlier age,
How at old Assyria's feet
Pilgrims from all lands would meet!

Yet when Egypt's self was young,
And Assyria's bloom unworn,
Ere the mythic Homer sung,
Ere the gods of Greece were born,
Lived the nation of one God,
Priests of freedom, sons of Shem,
Never quelled by yoke or rod,
Founders of Jerusalem
Is there one abides to-day,
Seeker of dead cities, say!

Answer, now as then, THEY ARE;
Scattered broadcast o'er the lands,
Knit in spirit nigh and far,
With indissoluble bands.
Half the world adores their God,
They the living law proclaim,
And their guerdon is the rod,
Stripes and scourgings, death and shame.
Still on Israel's head forlorn,
Every nation heaps its scorn.

August Moon

Look! the round-cheeked moon floats high,
In the glowing August sky,
Quenching all her neighbor stars,
Save the steady flame of Mars.
White as silver shines the sea,
Far-off sails like phantoms be,
Gliding o'er that lake of light,
Vanishing in nether night.
Heavy hangs the tasseled corn,
Sighing for the cordial morn;
But the marshy-meadows bare,
Love this spectral-lighted air,
Drink the dews and lift their song,

Chirp of crickets all night long;
Earth and sea enchanted lie
'Neath that moon-usurped sky.

To the faces of our friends
Unfamiliar traits she lends
Quaint, white witch, who looketh down
With a glamour all her own.
Hushed are laughter, jest, and speech,
Mute and heedless each of each,
In the glory wan we sit,
Visions vague before us flit;
Side by side, yet worlds apart,
Heart becometh strange to heart.

Slowly in a moved voice, then,
Ralph, the artist spake again
'Does not that weird orb unroll
Scenes phantasmal to your soul?
As I gaze thereon, I swear,
Peopled grows the vacant air,
Fables, myths alone are real,
White-clad sylph-like figures steal
'Twixt the bushes, o'er the lawn,
Goddess, nymph, undine, and faun.
Yonder, see the Willis dance,
Faces pale with stony glance;
They are maids who died unwed,
And they quit their gloomy bed,
Hungry still for human pleasure,
Here to trip a moonlit measure.
Near the shore the mermaids play,
Floating on the cool, white spray,
Leaping from the glittering surf
To the dark and fragrant turf,
Where the frolic trolls, and elves
Daintily disport themselves.
All the shapes by poet's brain,
Fashioned, live for me again,
In this spiritual light,
Less than day, yet more than night.
What a world! a waking dream,
All things other than they seem,
Borrowing a finer grace,
From yon golden globe in space;
Touched with wild, romantic glory,
Foliage fresh and billows hoary,
Hollows bathed in yellow haze,
Hills distinct and fields of maize,
Ancient legends come to mind.
Who would marvel should he find,

In the copse or nigh the spring,
Summer fairies gamboling
Where the honey-bees do suck,
Mab and Ariel and Puck?
Ah! no modern mortal sees
Creatures delicate as these.
All the simple faith has gone
Which their world was builded on.
Now the moonbeams coldly glance
On no gardens of romance;
To prosaic senses dull,
Baldur's dead, the Beautiful,
Hark, the cry rings overhead,
'Universal Pan is dead!"
'Requiescant!' Claude's grave tone
Thrilled us strangely. 'I am one
Who would not restore that Past,
Beauty will immortal last,
Though the beautiful must die
This the ages verify.
And had Pan deserved the name
Which his votaries misclaim,
He were living with us yet.
I behold, without regret,
Beauty in new forms recast,
Truth emerging from the vast,
Bright and orbed, like yonder sphere,
Making the obscure air clear.
He shall be of bards the king,
Who, in worthy verse, shall sing
All the conquests of the hour,
Stealing no fictitious power
From the classic types outworn,
But his rhythmic line adorn
With the marvels of the real.
He the baseless feud shall heal
That estrangeth wide apart
Science from her sister Art.
Hold! look through this glass for me?
Artist, tell me what you see?'
'I!' cried Ralph. 'I see in place
Of Astarte's silver face,
Or veiled Isis' radiant robe,
Nothing but a rugged globe
Seamed with awful rents and scars.
And below no longer Mars,
Fierce, flame-crested god of war,
But a lurid, flickering star,
Fashioned like our mother earth,
Vexed, belike, with death and birth.'

Rapt in dreamy thought the while,
With a sphinx-like shadowy smile,
Poet Florio sat, but now
Spake in deep-voiced accents slow,
More as one who probes his mind,
Than for us 'Who seeks, shall find
Widening knowledge surely brings
Vaster themes to him who sings.
Was veiled Isis more sublime
Than yon frozen fruit of Time,
Hanging in the naked sky?
Death's domain for worlds too die.
Lo! the heavens like a scroll
Stand revealed before my soul;
And the hieroglyphs are suns
Changeless change the law that runs
Through the flame-inscribed page,
World on world and age on age,
Balls of ice and orbs of fire,
What abides when these expire?
Through slow cycles they revolve,
Yet at last like clouds dissolve.
Jove, Osiris, Brahma pass,
Races wither like the grass.
Must not mortals be as gods
To embrace such periods?
Yet at Nature's heart remains
One who waxes not nor wanes.
And our crowning glory still
Is to have conceived his will.'

The South

Night, and beneath star-blazoned summer skies
Behold the Spirit of the musky South,
A creole with still-burning, languid eyes,
Voluptuous limbs and incense-breathing mouth:
Swathed in spun gauze is she,
From fibres of her own anana tree.

Within these sumptuous woods she lies at ease,
By rich night-breezes, dewy cool, caressed:
'Twixt cypresses and slim palmetto trees,
Like to the golden oriole's hanging nest,
Her airy hammock swings,
And through the dark her mocking-bird yet sings.

How beautiful she is! A tulip-wreath
Twines round her shadowy, free-floating hair:

Young, weary, passionate, and sad as death,
Dark visions haunt for her the vacant air,
While movelessly she lies
With lithe, lax, folded hands and heavy eyes.

Full well knows she how wide and fair extend
Her groves bright-flowered, her tangled everglades,
Majestic streams that indolently wend
Through lush savanna or dense forest shades,
Where the brown buzzard flies
To broad bayou 'neath hazy-golden skies.

Hers is the savage splendor of the swamp,
With pomp of scarlet and of purple bloom,
Where blow warm, furtive breezes faint and damp,
Strange insects whir, and stalking bitterns boom
Where from stale waters dead
Oft looms the great-jawed alligator's head.

Her wealth, her beauty, and the blight on these,
Of all she is aware: luxuriant woods,
Fresh, living, sunlit, in her dream she sees;
And ever midst those verdant solitudes
The soldier's wooden cross,
O'ergrown by creeping tendrils and rank moss.

Was her a dream of empire? was it sin?
And is it well that all was borne in vain?
She knows no more than one who slow doth win,
After fierce fever, conscious life again,
Too tired, too weak, too sad,
By the new light to be stirred or glad.

From rich sea-islands fringing her green shore,
From broad plantations where swart freemen bend
Bronzed backs in willing labor, from her store
Of golden fruit, from stream, from town, ascend
Life-currents of pure health:
Her aims shall be subserved with boundless wealth.

Yet now how listless and how still she lies,
Like some half-savage, dusky Indian queen,
Rocked in her hammock 'neath her native skies,
With the pathetic, passive, broken mien
Of one who, sorely proved,
Great-souled, hath suffered much and much hath loved!

But look! along the wide-branched, dewy glade
Glimmers the dawn: the light palmetto-trees
And cypresses reissue from the shade,
And SHE hath wakened. Through clear air she sees

The pledge, the brightening ray,
And leaps from dreams to hail the coming day.

To R.W.E.

As when a father dies, his children draw
About the empty hearth, their loss to cheat
With uttered praise & love, & oft repeat
His all-familiar words with whispered awe.
The honored habit of his daily law,
Not for his sake, but theirs whose feeble feet
Need still that guiding lamp, whose faith, less sweet,
Misses that tempered patience without flaw,
So do we gather round thy vacant chair,
In thine own elm-roofed, amber-rivered town,
Master & Father! For the love we bear,
Not for thy fame's sake, do we weave this crown,
And feel thy presence in the sacred air,
Forbidding us to weep that thou art gone.

Gifts

'O World God, give me Wealth!' the Egyptian cried.
His prayer was granted. High as heaven, behold
Palace and Pyramid; the brimming tide
Of lavish Nile washed all his land with gold.
Armies of slaves toiled ant-wise at his feet,
World-circling traffic roared through mart and street,
His priests were gods, his spice-balmed kings enshrined,
Set death at naught in rock-ribbed charnels deep.
Seek Pharaoh's race to-day and ye shall find
Rust and the moth, silence and dusty sleep.

'O World God, give me beauty!' cried the Greek.
His prayer was granted. All the earth became
Plastic and vocal to his sense; each peak,
Each grove, each stream, quick with Promethean flame,
Peopled the world with imaged grace and light.
The lyre was his, and his the breathing might
Of the immortal marble, his the play
Of diamond-pointed thought and golden tongue.
Go seek the sun-shine race, ye find to-day
A broken column and a lute unstrung.

'O World God, give me Power!' the Roman cried.
His prayer was granted. The vast world was chained
A captive to the chariot of his pride.

The blood of myriad provinces was drained
To feed that fierce, insatiable red heart.
Invulnerably bulwarked every part
With serried legions and with close-meshed Code,
Within, the burrowing worm had gnawed its home,
A roofless ruin stands where once abode
The imperial race of everlasting Rome.

'O Godhead, give me Truth!' the Hebrew cried.
His prayer was granted; he became the slave
Of the Idea, a pilgrim far and wide,
Cursed, hated, spurned, and scourged with none to save.
The Pharaohs knew him, and when Greece beheld,
His wisdom wore the hoary crown of Eld.
Beauty he hath forsworn, and wealth and power.
Seek him to-day, and find in every land.
No fire consumes him, neither floods devour;
Immortal through the lamp within his hand.

Epochs

'The epochs of our life are not in the facts, but in the silent thought by the wayside as we walk.'
Emerson

I. Youth

Sweet empty sky of June without a stain,
Faint, gray-blue dewy mists on far-off hills,
Warm, yellow sunlight flooding mead and plain,
That each dark copse and hollow overfills;
The rippling laugh of unseen, rain-fed rills,
Weeds delicate-flowered, white and pink and gold,
A murmur and a singing manifold.

The gray, austere old earth renews her youth
With dew-lines, sunshine, gossamer, and haze.
How still she lies and dreams, and veils the truth,
While all is fresh as in the early days!
What simple things be these the soul to raise
To bounding joy, and make young pulses beat,
With nameless pleasure finding life so sweet.

On such a golden morning forth there floats,
Between the soft earth and the softer sky,
In the warm air adust with glistening motes,
The mystic winged and flickering butterfly,
A human soul, that hovers giddily
Among the gardens of earth's paradise,

Nor dreams of fairer fields or loftier skies.

II. Regret

Thin summer rain on grass and bush and hedge,
Reddening the road and deepening the green
On wide, blurred lawn, and in close-tangled sedge;
Veiling in gray the landscape stretched between
These low broad meadows and the pale hills seen
But dimly on the far horizon's edge.

In these transparent clouded, gentle skies,
Wherethrough the moist beams of the soft June sun
Might any moment break, no sorrow lies,
No note of grief in swollen brooks that run,
No hint of woe in this subdued, calm tone
Of all the prospect unto dreamy eyes.

Only a tender, unnamed half-regret
For the lost beauty of the gracious morn;
A yearning aspiration, fainter yet,
For brighter suns in joyous days unborn,
Now while brief showers ruffle grass and corn,
And all the earth lies shadowed, grave, and wet;

Space for the happy soul to pause again
From pure content of all unbroken bliss,
To dream the future void of grief and pain,
And muse upon the past, in reveries
More sweet for knowledge that the present is
Not all complete, with mist and clouds and rain.

III. Longing

Look westward o'er the steaming rain-washed slopes,
Now satisfied with sunshine, and behold
Those lustrous clouds, as glorious as our hopes,
Softened with feathery fleece of downy gold,
In all fantastic, huddled shapes uprolled,
Floating like dreams, and melting silently,
In the blue upper regions of pure sky.

The eye is filled with beauty, and the heart
Rejoiced with sense of life and peace renewed;
And yet at such an hour as this, upstart
Vague myriad longing, restless, unsubdued,
And causeless tears from melancholy mood,
Strange discontent with earth's and nature's best,
Desires and yearnings that may find no rest.

IV. Storm

Serene was morning with clear, winnowed air,
But threatening soon the low, blue mass of cloud
Rose in the west, with mutterings faint and rare
At first, but waxing frequent and more loud.
Thick sultry mists the distant hill-tops shroud;
The sunshine dies; athwart black skies of lead
Flash noiselessly thin threads of lightning red.

Breathless the earth seems waiting some wild blow,
Dreaded, but far too close to ward or shun.
Scared birds aloft fly aimless, and below
Naught stirs in fields whence light and life are gone,
Save floating leaves, with wisps of straw and down,
Upon the heavy air; 'neath blue-black skies,
Livid and yellow the green landscape lies.

And all the while the dreadful thunder breaks,
Within the hollow circle of the hills,
With gathering might, that angry echoes wakes,
And earth and heaven with unused clamor fills.
O'erhead still flame those strange electric thrills.
A moment more, behold! yon bolt struck home,
And over ruined fields the storm hath come!

V. Surprise

When the stunned soul can first lift tired eyes
On her changed world of ruin, waste and wrack,
Ah, what a pang of aching sharp surprise
Brings all sweet memories of the lost past back,
With wild self-pitying grief of one betrayed,
Duped in a land of dreams where Truth is dead!

Are these the heavens that she deemed were kind?
Is this the world that yesterday was fair?
What painted images of folk half-blind
Be these who pass her by, as vague as air?
What go they seeking? there is naught to find.
Let them come nigh and hearken her despair.

A mocking lie is all she once believed,
And where her heart throbbed, is a cold dead stone.
This is a doom we never preconceived,
Yet now she cannot fancy it undone.
Part of herself, part of the whole hard scheme,
All else is but the shadow of a dream.

VI. Grief

There is a hungry longing in the soul,
A craving sense of emptiness and pain,
She may not satisfy nor yet control,
For all the teeming world looks void and vain.
No compensation in eternal spheres,
She knows the loneliness of all her years.

There is no comfort looking forth nor back,
The present gives the lie to all her past.
Will cruel time restore what she doth lack?
Why was no shadow of this doom forecast?
Ah! she hath played with many a keen-edged thing;
Naught is too small and soft to turn and sting.

In the unnatural glory of the hour,
Exalted over time, and death, and fate,
No earthly task appears beyond her power,
No possible endurance seemeth great.
She knows her misery and her majesty,
And recks not if she be to live or die.

VII. Acceptance

Yea, she hath looked Truth grimly face to face,
And drained unto the lees the proffered cup.
This silence is not patience, nor the grace
Of recognition, meekly offered up,
But mere acceptance fraught with keenest pain,
Seeing that all her struggles must be vain.

Her future clear and terrible outlies,
This burden to be borne through all her days,
This crown of thorns pressed down above her eyes,
This weight of trouble she may never raise.
No reconcilement doth she ask nor wait;
Knowing such things are, she endures her fate.

No brave endeavor of the broken will
To cling to such poor stays as will abide
(Although the waves be wild and angry still)
After the lapsing of the swollen tide.
No fear of further loss, no hope of gain,
Naught but the apathy of weary pain.

VIII. Loneliness

All stupor of surprise hath passed away;
She sees, with clearer vision than before,
A world far off of light and laughter gay,
Herself alone and lonely evermore.
Folk come and go, and reach her in no wise,
Mere flitting phantoms to her heavy eyes.

All outward things, that once seemed part of her,
Fall from her, like the leaves in autumn shed.
She feels as one embalmed in spice and myrrh,
With the heart eaten out, a long time dead;
Unchanged without, the features and the form;
Within, devoured by the thin red worm.

By her own prowess she must stand or fall,
This grief is to be conquered day by day.
Who could befriend her? who could make this small,
Or her strength great? she meets it as she may.
A weary struggle and a constant pain,
She dreams not they may ever cease nor wane.

IX. Sympathy

It comes not in such wise as she had deemed,
Else might she still have clung to her despair.
More tender, grateful than she could have dreamed,
Fond hands passed pitying over brows and hair,
And gentle words borne softly through the air,
Calming her weary sense and wildered mind,
By welcome, dear communion with her kind.

Ah! she forswore all words as empty lies;
What speech could help, encourage, or repair?
Yet when she meets these grave, indulgent eyes,
Fulfilled with pity, simplest words are fair,
Caressing, meaningless, that do not dare
To compensate or mend, but merely soothe
With hopeful visions after bitter Truth.

One who through conquered trouble had grown wise,
To read the grief unspoken, unexpressed,
The misery of the blank and heavy eyes,
Or through youth's infinite compassion guessed
The heavy burden, such a one brought rest,
And bade her lay aside her doubts and fears,
While the hard pain dissolved in blessed tears.

X. Patience

The passion of despair is quelled at last;
The cruel sense of undeserved wrong,
The wild self-pity, these are also past;
She knows not what may come, but she is strong;
She feels she hath not aught to lose nor gain,
Her patience is the essence of all pain.

As one who sits beside a lapsing stream,
She sees the flow of changeless day by day,
Too sick and tired to think, too sad to dream,
Nor cares how soon the waters slip away,
Nor where they lead; at the wise God's decree,
She will depart or bide indifferently.

There is deeper pathos in the mild
And settled sorrow of the quiet eyes,
Than in the tumults of the anguish wild,
That made her curse all things beneath the skies;
No question, no reproaches, no complaint,
Hers is the holy calm of some meek saint.

XI. Hope

Her languid pulses thrill with sudden hope,
That will not be forgot nor cast aside,
And life in statelier vistas seems to ope,
Illimitably lofty, long, and wide.
What doth she know? She is subdued and mild,
Quiet and docile 'as a weaned child.'

If grief came in such unimagined wise,
How may joy dawn? In what undreamed of hour,
May the light break with splendor of surprise,
Disclosing all the mercy and the power?
A baseless hope, yet vivid, keen, and bright,
As the wild lightning in the starless night.

She knows not whence it came, nor where it passed,
But it revealed, in one brief flash of flame,
A heaven so high, a world so rich and vast,
That, full of meek contrition and mute shame,
In patient silence hopefully withdrawn,
She bows her head, and bides the certain dawn.

XII. Compensation

'T is not alone that black and yawning void
That makes her heart ache with this hungry pain,

But the glad sense of life hath been destroyed,
The lost delight may never come again.
Yet myriad serious blessings with grave grace
Arise on every side to fill their place.

For much abides in her so lonely life,
The dear companionship of her own kind,
Love where least looked for, quiet after strife,
Whispers of promise upon every wind,
A quickened insight, in awakened eyes,
For the new meaning of the earth and skies.

The nameless charm about all things hath died,
Subtle as aureole round a shadow's head,
Cast on the dewy grass at morning-tide;
Yet though the glory and the joy be fled,
'T is much her own endurance to have weighed,
And wrestled with God's angels, unafraid.

XIII. Faith

She feels outwearied, as though o'er her head
A storm of mighty billows broke and passed.
Whose hand upheld her? Who her footsteps led
To this green haven of sweet rest at last?
What strength was hers, unreckoned and unknown?
What love sustained when she was most alone?

Unutterably pathetic her desire,
To reach, with groping arms outstretched in prayer,
Something to cling to, to uplift her higher
From this low world of coward fear and care,
Above disaster, that her will may be
At one with God's, accepting his decree.

Though by no reasons she be justified,
Yet strangely brave in Evil's very face,
She deems this want must needs be satisfied,
Though here all slips from out her weak embrace.
And in blind ecstasy of perfect faith,
With her own dream her prayer she answereth.

XIV. Work

Yet life is not a vision nor a prayer,
But stubborn work; she may not shun her task.
After the first compassion, none will spare
Her portion and her work achieved, to ask.
She pleads for respite, she will come ere long

When, resting by the roadside, she is strong.

Nay, for the hurrying throng of passers-by
Will crush her with their onward-rolling stream.
Much must be done before the brief light die;
She may not loiter, rapt in the vain dream.
With unused trembling hands, and faltering feet,
She staggers forth, her lot assigned to meet.

But when she fills her days with duties done,
Strange vigor comes, she is restored to health.
New aims, new interests rise with each new sun,
And life still holds for her unbounded wealth.
All that seemed hard and toilsome now proves small,
And naught may daunt her, she hath strength for all.

XV. Victory

How strange, in some brief interval of rest,
Backward to look on her far-stretching past.
To see how much is conquered and repressed,
How much is gained in victory at last!
The shadow is not lifted, but her faith,
Strong from life's miracles, now turns toward death.

Though much be dark where once rare splendor shone,
Yet the new light has touched high peaks unguessed
In her gold, mist-bathed dawn, and one by one
New outlooks loom from many a mountain crest.
She breathes a loftier, purer atmosphere,
And life's entangled paths grow straight and clear.

Nor will Death prove an all-unwelcome guest;
The struggle has been toilsome to this end,
Sleep will be sweet, and after labor rest,
And all will be atoned with him to friend.
Much must be reconciled, much justified,
And yet she feels she will be satisfied.

XVI. Peace

The calm outgoing of a long, rich day,
Checkered with storm and sunshine, gloom and light,
Now passing in pure, cloudless skies away,
Withdrawing into silence of blank night.
Thick shadows settle on the landscape bright,
Like the weird cloud of death that falls apace
On the still features of the passive face.

Soothing and gentle as a mother's kiss,
The touch that stopped the beating of the heart.
A look so blissfully serene as this,
Not all the joy of living could impart.
With dauntless faith and courage therewithal,
The Master found her ready at his call.

On such a golden evening forth there floats,
Between the grave earth and the glowing sky
In the clear air, unvexed with hazy motes,
The mystic-winged and flickering butterfly,
A human soul, that drifts at liberty,
Ah! who can tell to what strange paradise,
To what undreamed of fields and lofty skies!

Mater Amabilis

Down the goldenest of streams,
Tide of dreams,
The fair cradled man-child drifts;
Sways with cadenced motion slow,
To and fro,
As the mother-foot poised lightly, falls and lifts.

He, the firstling, he, the light
Of her sight,
He, the breathing pledge of love,
'Neath the holy passion lies,
Of her eyes,
Smiles to feel the warm, life-giving ray above.

She believes that in his vision,
Skies elysian
O'er an angel-people shine.
Back to gardens of delight,
Taking flight,
His auroral spirit basks in dreams divine.

But she smiles through anxious tears;
Unborn years
Pressing forward, she perceives.
Shadowy muffled shapes, they come
Deaf and dumb,
Bringing what? dry chaff and tares, or full eared sheaves?

What for him shall she invoke?
Shall the oak
Bind the man's triumphant brow?
Shall his daring foot alight

On the height?
Shall he dwell amidst the humble and the low?

Through what tears and sweat and pain,
Must he gain
Fruitage from the tree of life?
Shall it yield him bitter flavor?
Shall its savor
Be as manna midst the turmoil and the strife?

In his cradle slept and smiled
Thus the child
Who as Prince of Peace was hailed.
Thus anigh the mother breast,
Lulled to rest,
Child-Napoleon down the lilied river sailed.

Crowned or crucified the same
Glows the flame
Of her deathless love divine.
Still the blessed mother stands,
In all lands,
As she watched beside thy cradle and by mine.

Whatso gifts the years bestow,
Still men know,
While she breathes, lives one who sees
(Stand they pure or sin-defiled)
But the child
Whom she crooned to sleep and rocked upon her knee.

The Birth Of Man

A Legend of the Talmud.

I.
When angels visit earth, the messengers
Of God's decree, they come as lightning, wind:
Before the throne, they all are living fire.
There stand four rows of angels to the right
The hosts of Michael, Gabriel's to the left,
Before, the troop of Ariel, and behind,
The ranks of Raphael; all, with one accord,
Chanting the glory of the Everlasting.
Upon the high and holy throne there rests,
Invisible, the Majesty of God.
About his brows the crown of mystery
Whereon the sacred letters are engraved
Of the unutterable Name. He grasps

A sceptre of keen fire; the universe
Is compassed in His glance; at His right hand
Life stands, and at His left hand standeth Death.

II.
Lo, the divine idea of making man
Had spread abroad among the heavenly hosts;
And all at once before the immortal throne
Pressed troops of angels and of seraphim,
With minds opposed, and contradicting cries:
'Fulfill, great Father, thine exalted thought!
Create and give unto the earth her king!'
'Cease, cease, Almighty God! create no more!'
And suddenly upon the heavenly sphere
Deep silence fell; before the immortal throne
The angel Mercy knelt, and thus he spoke:
'Fulfill, great Father, thine exalted thought!
Create the likeness of thyself on earth.
In this new creature I will breathe the spirit
Of a divine compassion; he shall be
Thy fairest image in the universe.'
But to his words the angel Peace replied,
With heavy sobs: 'My spirit was outspread,
Oh God, on thy creation, and all things
Were sweetly bound in gracious harmony.
But man, this strange new being, everywhere
Shall bring confusion, trouble, discord, war.'
'Avenger of injustice and of crime,'
Exclaimed the angel Justice, 'he shall be
Subject to me, and peace shall bloom again.
Create, oh Lord, create!' 'Father of truth,'
Implored with tears the angel Truth, 'Thou bring'st
Upon the earth the father of all lies!'
And over the celestial faces gloomed
A cloud of grief, and stillness deep prevailed.
Then from the midst of that abyss of light
Whence sprang the eternal throne, these words rang forth:
'Be comforted, my daughter! Thee I send
To be companion unto man on earth.'
And all the angels cried, lamenting loud:
'Thou robbest heaven of her fairest gem.
Truth! seal of all thy thoughts, Almighty God,
The richest jewel that adorns thy crown.'
From the abyss of glory rang the voice:
'From heaven to earth, from earth once more to heaven,
Shall Truth, with constant interchange, alight
And soar again, an everlasting link
Between the world and sky.'
And man was born.

Bar Kochba

Weep, Israel! your tardy meed outpour
Of grateful homage on his fallen head,
That never coronal of triumph wore,
Untombed, dishonored, and unchapleted.
If Victory makes the hero, raw Success
The stamp of virtue, unremembered
Be then the desperate strife, the storm and stress
Of the last Warrior Jew. But if the man
Who dies for freedom, loving all things less,
Against world legions, mustering his poor clan;
The weak, the wronged, the miserable, to send
Their death-cry's protest through the ages' span
If such an one be worthy, ye shall lend
Eternal thanks to him, eternal praise.
Nobler the conquered than the conqueror's end!

The Choice

I saw in dream the spirits unbegot,
Veiled, floating phantoms, lost in twilight space;
For one the hour had struck, he paused; the place
Rang with an awful Voice:
'Soul, choose thy lot!
Two paths are offered; that, in velvet-flower,
Slopes easily to every earthly prize.
Follow the multitude and bind thine eyes,
Thou and thy sons' sons shall have peace with power.
This narrow track skirts the abysmal verge,
Here shalt thou stumble, totter, weep and bleed,
All men shall hate and hound thee and thy seed,
Thy portion be the wound, the stripe, the scourge.
But in thy hand I place my lamp for light,
Thy blood shall be the witness of my Law,
Choose now for all the ages!'
Then I saw
The unveiled spirit, grown divinely bright,
Choose the grim path. He turned, I knew full well
The pale, great martyr-forehead shadowy-curled,
The glowing eyes that had renounced the world,
Disgraced, despised, immortal Israel.

The Valley Of Baca

PSALM LXXXIV.

A brackish lake is there with bitter pools
Anigh its margin, brushed by heavy trees.
A piping wind the narrow valley cools,
Fretting the willows and the cypresses.
Gray skies above, and in the gloomy space
An awful presence hath its dwelling-place.

I saw a youth pass down that vale of tears;
His head was circled with a crown of thorn,
His form was bowed as by the weight of years,
His wayworn feet by stones were cut and torn.
His eyes were such as have beheld the sword
Of terror of the angel of the Lord.

He passed, and clouds and shadows and thick haze
Fell and encompassed him. I might not see
What hand upheld him in those dismal ways,
Wherethrough he staggered with his misery.
The creeping mists that trooped and spread around,
The smitten head and writhing form enwound.

Then slow and gradual but sure they rose,
Those clinging vapors blotting out the sky.
The youth had fallen not, his viewless foes
Discomfited, had left the victory
Unto the heart that fainted not nor failed,
But from the hill-tops its salvation hailed.

I looked at him in dread lest I should see,
The anguish of the struggle in his eyes;
And lo, great peace was there! Triumphantly
The sunshine crowned him from the sacred skies.
'From strength to strength he goes,' he leaves beneath
The valley of the shadow and of death.

'Thrice blest who passing through that vale of Tears,
Makes it a well,' and draws life-nourishment
From those death-bitter drops. No grief, no fears
Assail him further, he may scorn the event.
For naught hath power to swerve the steadfast soul
Within that valley broken and made whole.

Links

The little and the great are joined in one
By God's great force. The wondrous golden sun
Is linked unto the glow-worm's tiny spark;

The eagle soars to heaven in his flight;
And in those realms of space, all bathed in light,
Soar none except the eagle and the lark.

Youth And Death

What hast thou done to this dear friend of mine,
Thou cold, white, silent Stranger? From my hand
Her clasped hand slips to meet the grasp of thine;
Here eyes that flamed with love, at thy command
Stare stone-blank on blank air; her frozen heart
Forgets my presence. Teach me who thou art,
Vague shadow sliding 'twixt my friend and me.
I never saw thee till this sudden hour.
What secret door gave entrance unto thee?
What power in thine, o'ermastering Love's own power?

Spring Longing

Lilac hazes veil the skies.
Languid sighs
Breathes the mild, caressing air.
Pink as coral's branching sprays,
Orchard ways
With the blossomed peach are fair.

Sunshine, cordial as a kiss,
Poureth bliss
In this craving soul of mine,
And my heart her flower-cup
Lifteth up,
Thirsting for the draught divine.

Swift the liquid golden flame
Through my frame
Sets my throbbing veins afire.
Bright, alluring dreams arise,
Brim mine eyes
With the tears of strong desire.

All familiar scenes anear
Disappear
Homestead, orchard, field, and wold.
Moorish spires and turrets fair
Cleave the air,
Arabesqued on skies of gold.

Low, my spirit, this May morn,
Outward borne,
Over seas hath taken wing:
Where the mediaeval town,
Like a crown,
Wears the garland of the Spring.

Light and sound and odors sweet
Fill the street;
Gypsy girls are selling flowers.
Lean hidalgos turn aside,
Amorous-eyed,
'Neath the grim cathedral towers.

Oh, to be in Spain to-day,
Where the May
Recks no whit of good or evil,
Love and only love breathes she!
Oh, to be
'Midst the olive-rows of Seville!

Or on such a day to glide
With the tide
Of the berylline lagoon,
Through the streets that mirror heaven,
Crystal paven,
In the warm Venetian noon.

At the prow the gondolier
May not hear,
May not see our furtive kiss;
But he lends with cadenced strain
The refrain
To our ripe and silent bliss.

Golden shadows, silver light,
Burnish bright
Air and water, domes and skies;
As in some ambrosial dream,
On the stream
Floats our bark in magic wise.

Oh, to float day long just so!
Naught to know
Of the trouble, toil, and fret!
This is love, and this is May:
Yesterday
And to-morrow to forget!

Whither hast thou, Fancy free,
Guided me,

Wild Bohemian sister dear?
All thy gypsy soul is stirred
Since yon bird
Warbled that the Spring was here.

Tempt no more! I may not follow,
Like the swallow,
Gayly on the track of Spring.
Bounden by an iron fate,
I must wait,
Dream and wonder, yearn and sing.

Spring Star

I.
Over the lamp-lit street,
Trodden by hurrying feet,
Where mostly pulse and beat
Life's throbbing veins,
See where the April star,
Blue-bright as sapphires are,
Hangs in deep heavens far,
Waxes and wanes.

Strangely alive it seems,
Darting keen, dazzling gleams,
Veiling anon its beams,
Large, clear, and pure.
In the broad western sky
No orb may shine anigh,
No lesser radiancy
May there endure.

Spring airs are blowing sweet:
Low in the dusky street
Star-beams and eye-beams meet.
Rapt in his dreams,
All through the crowded mart
Poet with swift-stirred heart,
Passing beneath, must start,
Thrilled by those gleams.

Naught doth he note anear,
Fain through Night's veil to peer,
Reach that resplendent sphere,
Reading her sign.
Where point those sharp, thin rays,
Guiding his weary maze,
Blesseth she or betrays,

Who may divine?

'Guard me, celestial light,
Lofty, serenely bright:
Lead my halt feet aright,'
Prayerful he speaks.
'For a new ray hath shone
Over my spirit lone.
Be this new soul the one
whom my soul seeks.'

II.
Beside her casement oped the maiden sits,
Where the mild evening spirit of the Spring
Gently between the city's homesteads flits
To kiss her brows, and floats on languid wing,
Vague longings in her breast awakening.
While her heart trembles 'neath those dim, deep skies,
As the quick sea that 'neath the globed moon lies.

Where her eyes rest the full-orbed evening star
Burns with white flame: it beckons, shrinks, dilates.
She, dazzled by that shining world afar,
May not withdraw her gaze: breathless she waits.
Some promised joy from Heaven's very gates
Unto her soul seems proffered. When shall be
The bright fulfilment of that star's decree?

Nor glad nor sad is she: she doth not know
That through the city's throng one threads his way,
Thrilled likewise by that planet's mystic glow,
And hastes to seek her. What sweet change shall sway
Her spirit at his coming? What new ray
Upon his shadowy life from her shall fall?
The silent star burns on, and knoweth all.

Song

Venus.

Frosty lies the winter landscape,
In the twilight golden green.
Down the Park's deserted alleys,
Naked elms stand stark and lean.

Dumb the murmur of the fountain,
Birds have flown from lawn and hill.
But while yonder star's ascendant,

Love triumphal reigneth still.

See the keen flame throb and tremble,
Brightening in the darkening night,
Breathing like a thing of passion,
In the sky's smooth chrysolite.

Not beneath the moon, oh lover,
Thou shalt gain thy heart's desire.
Speak to-night! The gods are with thee
Burning with a kindred fire.

Sunrise

Weep for the martyr! Strew his bier
With the last roses of the year;
Shadow the land with sables; knell
The harsh-tongued, melancholy bell;
Beat the dull muffled drum, and flaunt
The drooping banner; let the chant
Of the deep-throated organ sob
One voice, one sorrow, one heart-throb,
From land to land, from sea to sea
The huge world quires his elegy.
Tears, love, and honor he shall have,
Through ages keeping green his grave.
Too late approved, too early lost,
His story is the people's boast.
Tough-sinewed offspring of the soil,
Of peasant lineage, reared to toil,
In Europe he had been a thing
To the glebe tethered here a king!
Crowned not for some transcendent gift,
Genius of power that may lift
A Caesar or a Bonaparte
Up to the starred goal of his heart;
But that he was the epitome
Of all the people aim to be.
Were they his dying trust? He was
No less their model and their glass.
In him the daily traits were viewed
Of the undistinguished multitude.
Brave as the silent myriads are,
Crushed by the juggernaut world-car;
Strong with the people's strength, yet mild,
Simple and tender as a child;
Wise with the wisdom of the heart,
Able in council, field, and mart;
Nor lacking in the lambent gleam,

The great soul's final stamp the beam
Of genial fun, the humor sane
Wherewith the hero sports with pain.
His virtues hold within the span
Of his obscurest fellow-man.
To live without reproach, to die
Without a fear in these words lie
His highest aims, for none too high.
No triumph his beyond the reach
Of patient courage, kindly speech;
And yet so brave the soul outbreathed,
The great example he bequeathed,
Were all to follow, we should see
A universal chivalry.

His trust, the People! They respond
From Maine to Florida, beyond
The sea-walled continent's broad scope,
Honor his pledge, confirm his hope.
Hark! over seas the echo hence,
The nations do him reverence.
An Empress lays her votive wreath
Where peoples weep with bated breath.
The world-clock strikes a fateful hour,
Bright with fair portents, big with power,
The first since history's course has run,
When kings' and peoples' cause is one;
Those mourn a brother these a son!

O how he loved them! That gray morn,
When his wound-wasted form was borne
North, from the White House to the sea,
Lifting his tired lids thankfully,
'How good,' he murmured in his pain,
'To see the people once again!'
Oh, how they loved him! They stood there,
Thronging the road, the street, the square,
With hushed lips locked in silent prayer,
Uncovered heads and streaming eyes,
Breathless as when a father dies.
The records of the ghostly ride,
Past town and field at morning-tide.

When life's full stream is wont to gush
Through all its ways with boisterous rush,
The records note that once a hound
Had barked, and once was heard the sound
Of cart-wheels rumbling on the stones
And once, mid stifled sobs and groans,
One man dared audibly lament,
And cried, 'God bless the president!'

Always the waiting crowds to send
A God-speed to his journey's end
The anxious whisper, brow of gloom,
As in a sickness-sacred room,
Till his ear drank with ecstasy
The rhythmic thunders of the sea.

Tears for the smitten fatherless,
The wife's, the mother's life-distress,
To whom the million-throated moan
From throne and hut, may not atone
For one hushed voice, one empty chair,
One presence missing everywhere.
But only words of joy and sheer,
The people from his grave shall hear.
Were they not worthy of his trust,
From whose seed sprang the sacred dust?
He broke the bars that separate
The humble from the high estate.
And heirs of empire round his bed
Mourn with the 'disinherited.'

Oh, toil-worn, patient Heart that bleeds,
Whose martyrdom even his exceeds,
Wronged, cursed, despised, misunderstood
Oh, all-enduring multitude,
Rejoice! amid you tears, rejoice!
There issues from this grave a voice,
Proclaiming your long night is o'er,
Your day-dawn breaks from shore to shore.
You have redeemed his pledge, remained
Secure, erect, and self-sustained,
Holding more dear one thing alone,
Even than the blood of dearest son,
Revering with religious awe
The inviolable might of Law.

Fra Pedro

Golden lights and lengthening shadows,
Flings the splendid sun declining,
O'er the monastery garden
Rich in flower, fruit and foliage.

Through the avenue of nut trees,
Pace two grave and ghostly friars,
Snowy white their gowns and girdles,
Black as night their cowls and mantles.

Lithe and ferret-eyed the younger,
Black his scapular denoting
A lay brother; his companion
Large, imperious, towers above him.

'T is the abbot, great Fra Pedro,
Famous through all Saragossa
For his quenchless zeal in crushing
Heresy amidst his townfolk.

Handsome still with hood and tonsure,
E'en as when the boy Pedrillo,
Insolent with youth and beauty,
Who reviled the gentle Rabbi.

Lo, the level sun strikes sparkles
From his dark eyes brightly flashing.
Stern his voice: 'These too shall perish.
I have vowed extermination.

'Tell not me of skill or virtue,
Filial love or woman's beauty
Jews are Jews, as serpents serpents,
In themselves abomination.'

Earnestly the other pleaded,
'If my zeal, thrice reverend master,
E'er afforded thee assistance,
Serving thee as flesh serves spirit,

'Hounding, scourging, flaying, burning,
Casting into chains or exile,
At thy bidding these vile wretches,
Hear and heed me now, my master.

'These be nowise like their brethren,
Ben Jehudah is accounted
Saragossa's first physician,
Loved by colleague as by patient.

'And his daughter Donna Zara
Is our city's pearl of beauty,
Like the clusters of the vineyard
Droop the ringlets o'er her temples.

'Like the moon in starry heavens
Shines her face among her people,
And her form hath all the languor,
Grace and glamour of the palm-tree.

'Well thou knowest, thrice reverend master,

This is not their first affliction,
Was it not our Holy Office
Whose bribed menials fired their dwelling?

'Ere dawn broke, the smoke ascended,
Choked the stairways, filled the chambers,
Waked the household to the terror
Of the flaming death that threatened.

'Then the poor bed-ridden mother
Knew her hour had come; two daughters,
Twinned in form, and mind, and spirit,
And their father who would save them?

'Towards her door sprang Ben Jehudah,
Donna Zara flew behind him
Round his neck her white arms wreathing,
Drew him from the burning chamber.

'There within, her sister Zillah
Stirred no limb to shun her torture,
Held her mother's hand and kissed her,
Saying, 'We will go together.'

'This the outer throng could witness,
As the flames enwound the dwelling,
Like a glory they illumined
Awfully the martyred daughter.

'Closer, fiercer, round they gathered,
Not a natural cry escaped her,
Helpless clung to her her mother,
Hand in hand they went together.

'Since that 'Act of Faith' three winters
Have rolled by, yet on the forehead
Of Jehudah is imprinted
Still the horror of that morning.

'Saragossa hath respected
His false creed; a man of sorrows,
He hath walked secure among us,
And his art repays our sufferance.'

Thus he spoke and ceased. The Abbot
Lent him an impatient hearing,
Then outbroke with angry accent,
'We have borne three years, thou sayest?

"T is enough; my vow is sacred.
These shall perish with their brethren.

Hark ye! In my veins' pure current
Were a single drop found Jewish,

'I would shrink not from outpouring
All my life blood, but to purge it.
Shall I gentler prove to others?
Mercy would be sacrilegious.

'Ne'er again at thy soul's peril,
Speak to me of Jewish beauty,
Jewish skill, or Jewish virtue.
I have said. Do thou remember.'

Down behind the purple hillside
Dropped the sun; above the garden
Rang the Angelus' clear cadence
Summoning the monks to vespers.

Don Rafael

'I would not have,' he said,
'Tears, nor the black pall, nor the wormy grave,
Grief's hideous panoply I would not have
Round me when I am dead.

'Music and flowers and light,
And choric dances to guitar and flute,
Be these around me when my lips are mute,
Mine eyes are sealed from sight.

'So let me lie one day,
One long, eternal day, in sunshine bathed,
In cerements of silken tissue swathed,
Smothered 'neath flowers of May.

'One perfect day of peace,
Or ere clean flame consume my fleshly veil,
My life - a gilded vapor - shall exhale,
Brief as a sigh and cease.

'But ere the torch be laid
To my unshrinking limbs by some true hand,
Athwart the orange-fragrant laughing land,
Bring many a dark-eyed maid

'From the bright, sea-kissed town;
My beautiful, beloved enemies,
Gemmed as the dew, voluptuous as the breeze,
Each in her festal gown.

'All those through whom I learned
The sweet of folly and the pains of love,
My Rose, my Star, my Comforter, my Dove,
For whom, poor moth, I burned.

'Loves of a day, and hour,
Or passions (vowed eternal) of a year,
Though each be strange to each, to me all dear
As to the bee the flower.

'Around me they shall move
In languid contra dances, and shall shed
Their smiling eyebeams as I were not dead,
But quick to flash back love.

'Something not alien quite
To tender ruth, perchance their breast shall fill,
Seeing him that was so mobile grown so still,
The fiery-veined so white.

'And when the dance is o'er,
The pinched guitar, the smitten tambourine,
Have ceased their rhythmic beat, oh, friends of mine,
On my rich bier, then pour

'The garlands that ye wear,
The happy rose that on your bosom breathes,
The fresh-culled clusters and the dewy wreaths
That crown your fragrant hair.

'Though blind, I still shall see,
Though dead, shall feel your presence and shall know,
I who was beauty's life-long slave, shall so
Win her in death to me.

'Thanks, sisters, and farewell!
Back to your joys. My brother shall make room
For my tried sword upon the high-piled bloom,
And fire the pinnacle.

'My soul, pure flame, shall leap
To meet its parent essence once again
My body dust and ashes shall remain,
Tired heart and brain shall sleep.

'Life has one gate alone,
Obscure, beset with peril and fierce pain.
Large death has many portals to his fane,
Why choose we to make moan?

'Why dwell with worms and clay
When we may soar through air on wings of flame,
Dissolve to small, white dust our perfect frame,
And never know decay?

'A brother's pious hand
The pure, fire-winnowed ashes shall inurn,
And lay them in the orange grove where burn
Globed suns that scent the land.

'The leaf shall be more green,
Even for my dust, more snowy, soft the flower,
More juicy-sweet the fruit's live pulp the bower
Richer that I have been.

'For I would not,' he said,
'Tears and the black pall and the wormy grave,
Grief's hideous panoply I would not have
Round me when I am dead.'

To Carmen Sylva

Oh, that the golden lyre divine
Whence David smote flame-tones were mine!
Oh, that the silent harp which hung
Untuned, unstrung,
Upon the willows by the river,
Would throb beneath my touch and quiver
With the old song-enchanted spell
Of Israel!

Oh, that the large prophetic Voice
Would make my reed-piped throat its choice!
All ears should prick, all hearts should spring,
To hear me sing
The burden of the isles, the word
Assyria knew, Damascus heard,
When, like the wind, while cedars shake,
Isaiah spake.

For I would frame a song to-day
Winged like a bird to cleave its way
O'er land and sea that spread between,
To where a Queen
Sits with a triple coronet.
Genius and Sorrow both have set
Their diadems above the gold
A Queen three-fold!

To her the forest lent its lyre,
Hers are the sylvan dews, the fire
Of Orient suns, the mist-wreathed gleams
Of mountain streams.
She, the imperial Rhine's own child,
Takes to her heart the wood-nymph wild,
The gypsy Pelech, and the wide,
White Danube's tide.

She who beside an infant's bier
Long since resigned all hope to hear
The sacred name of 'Mother' bless
Her childlessness,
Now from a people's sole acclaim
Receives the heart-vibrating name,
And 'Mother, Mother, Mother!' fills
The echoing hills.

Yet who is he who pines apart,
Estranged from that maternal heart,
Ungraced, unfriended, and forlorn,
The butt of scorn?
An alien in his land of birth,
An outcast from his brethren's earth,
Albeit with theirs his blood mixed well
When Plevna fell?

When all Roumania's chains were riven,
When unto all his sons was given
The hero's glorious reward,
Reaped by the sword,
Wherefore was this poor thrall, whose chains
Hung heaviest, within whose veins
The oldest blood of freedom streamed,
Still unredeemed?

O Mother, Poet, Queen in one!
Pity and save he is thy son.
For poet David's sake, the king
Of all who sing;
For thine own people's sake who share
His law, his truth, his praise, his prayer;
For his sake who was sacrificed
His brother - Christ!

The Banner Of The Jew

Wake, Israel, wake! Recall to-day
The glorious Maccabean rage,

The sire heroic, hoary-gray,
His five-fold lion-lineage:
The Wise, the Elect, the Help-of-God,
The Burst-of-Spring, the Avenging Rod.

From Mizpeh's mountain-ridge they saw
Jerusalem's empty streets, her shrine
Laid waste where Greeks profaned the Law,
With idol and with pagan sign.
Mourners in tattered black were there,
With ashes sprinkled on their hair.

Then from the stony peak there rang
A blast to ope the graves: down poured
The Maccabean clan, who sang
Their battle anthem to the Lord.
Five heroes lead, and following, see,
Ten thousand rush to victory!

Oh for Jerusalem's trumpet now,
To blow a blast of shattering power,
To wake the sleepers high and low,
And rouse them to the urgent hour!
No hand for vengeance but to save,
A million naked swords should wave.

Oh deem not dead that martial fire,
Say not the mystic flame is spent!
With Moses' law and David's lyre,
Your ancient strength remains unbent.
Let but an Ezra rise anew,
To lift the BANNER OF THE JEW!

A rag, a mock at first erelong,
When men have bled and women wept,
To guard its precious folds from wrong,
Even they who shrunk, even they who slept,
Shall leap to bless it, and to save.
Strike! for the brave revere the brave!

Sic Semper Liberatoribus!

As one who feels the breathless nightmare grip
His heart-strings, and through visioned horrors fares,
Now on a thin-ledged chasm's rock-crumbling lip,
Now on a tottering pinnacle that dare
The front of heaven, while always unawares
Weird monsters start above, around, beneath,
Each glaring from some uglier mask of death,

So the White Czar imperial progress made
Through terror-haunted days. A shock, a cry
Whose echoes ring the globe - the spectre's laid.
Hurled o'er the abyss, see the crowned martyr lie
Resting in peace-fear, change, and death gone by.
Fit end for nightmare mist of blood and tears,
Red climax to the slow, abortive years.

The world draws breath, one long, deep-shuddering sigh,
At that which dullest brain prefigured clear
As swift-sure bolt from thunder-threatening sky.
How heaven-anointed humblest lots appear
Beside his glittering eminence of fear;
His spiked crown, sackcloth purple, poisoned cates,
His golden palace honey-combed with hates.

Well is it done! A most heroic plan,
Which after myriad plots succeeds at last
In robbing of his life this poor old man,
Whose sole offense - his birthright - has but passed
To fresher blood, with younger strength recast.
What men are these, who, clamoring to be free,
Would bestialize the world to what they be?

Whose sons are they who made the snow-wreathed head
Their frenzy's target? In their Russian veins,
What alien current urged on to smite him dead,
Whose word had loosed a million Russian chains?
What brutes were they for whom such speechless pains,
So royally endured, no human thrill
Awoke, in hearts drunk with the lust to kill?

Not brutes! No tiger of the wilderness,
No jackal of the jungle, bears such brand
As man's black heart, who shrinks not to confess
The desperate deed of his deliberate hand.
Our kind, our kin, have done this thing. We stand
Bowed earthward, red with shame, to see such wrong
Prorogue Love's cause and Truth's - God knows how long!

Made in the USA
San Bernardino, CA
09 March 2019